Astonished Birds

Cara, Jane, Bob and James.

Astonished Birds

Cara, Jane, Bob and James.

Catherine Walsh

hardPressed poetry

Published by hardPressed poetry

http://hardpressedpoetry.blogspot.com/
hardpressedpoetry@gmail.com

Cover design by hardPressed poetry with Maurice O'Connor

ISBN: 978-1-872781-05-1

Parts of this book were read at Béal Festival, Fingal's Writing 3.0 Festival and the White House, Limerick. Thank you to everybody.

shells from
strands
of lore

Perhaps it's the fish which
Astonished birds imagine
imagining imagined monologues on
aspects of art or

Perhaps Astonished birds are
the fish which imagine
imagining imagined monologues
on aspects of art or

Perhaps the fish which Astonished
birds imagine themselves being imagining imagined
monologues on aspects of art are

Perhaps Astonished birds imagining
imagining imagined monologues
on aspects of art so

Perhaps the fish which could imagine
imagining imagined monologues
on aspects of art and

Perhaps the fish which Astonished
birds imagine imagining are as
the astonished birds imagine imagining the
fish which imagined then

Perhaps it's the astonished fish which
imagining imagined birds imagining
imagined monologues on aspects
of art astonishes as

Perhaps the astonished fish which
astonished birds imagine
imagining imagined monologues on
aspects of art is as the fish which
Astonished birds imagine imagining so

Astonished birds monologues on
aspects of the fish which imagined
imagining aspects of art.

yr lost age of
magical transformation
listening
does not
hear   hearing
does
not listen while
past regallops issues
forth voids grace notes
mothers say do not open
doors
a scarring
pips
this
unexpected
not improbable
lot coming
across
weighing
floundering
(with) spaces
air
clears to
will o' the wisp
mist
lightness
missed

perturbed by light
its shapes
what's left out
searching each day
for spaces
of light
traceries demonstrating
quantity quality
duration density
absorption
going all the way
home this place by
likelihood light
potential showings spaces
juxtaposition of
particulate
matter dominating
route choice
stopping points

catching pictures
bouncing
refractions
negotiate in milli
seconds how
thick quivering
tentatively
interconnected
aerial expanses
threaten any
known solidity

tonal encompassing
of edge flexible
reiteration of
glint hardy
exposition
of plane

this is a
low sun high
by ten thirty
profoundly cold
spring start here
perhaps only four
or five more days
of clarity reason
to look

stopping points
of plane
to look
perturbed by light
catching the picture
this is a
home this place by
the tonal encompassing
look

shells from
strands
of lore
scattered
piled
placed
exactly

yore line echoing
threaded
rattled
conch shells
to ears
on the gravelled
verge round
the house low
concreted kerbs
retaining stone
trench dug
drainage infill
thwarting
victorian damp
decorated with
edwardian
exotic shells
wrought iron
wooden furniture
ceramic plantholders
glazed pots terracotta
stands of colour
the quietening

lair   see
sea   hear
shore line water
break shush
waves whush
 thump lands
 water   shush
 waves sea   see

early morning
conch shells
        steel bucket
of snails dewy
pollen stuck
bee trails

It is not inspiring. None of it. What is? Asking
that, opening portholes, moving levers. Of all the
content/subject matters always the
recurrence of [primal listing interspersed with a few more recent takes
on the concerns of material life] A minefield,
separating these. Inspiration, needs
reasonable respiration. Naturally possible there is no
freedom, only in perception glimpses; if even that is
choice? What is perception? How many senses form
a person's received bank of perceptive experiences? Experiential
memory. Going too far, fallacious, saying no freedom
but in memory. That parallel to dream states, the
inhabiting of mind, evolving formation, growth as sets
of strategies, perceptions, reactions, responses, reductions,
processes all. Memory is never actuality, tangible.
Experiential, emotional memory elicits a seemingly true core of
feeling, sympathy, empathy, even to the hearing perceptually,
perceptively in memory's store, of voices of the well-known dead
or geographically far distant, intimacy of knowing remains,
scents their scent. Triggered by memory's recesses, mind's
resources, changes in light formats, landscapes,
internal scenes: or by sounds heard through certain contexts, not
attended, processed as learnt in that situation. And on. All
noted documented before think of residual past cultures
as traceries of talent, scaffolding for skills.

The memory of light. As if it could be--? Representational?
Symbolic? Significant? Important? Necessary? Of course the
last three work straight away nature, the earth, life.
So are the previous two necessarily hybrids from what evolves of
that life allowed, chanced, happened, that accident or juxtaposition
of fortuities?

How far, anthropologically speaking, have we moved beyond
the seeking thinking of the motivated survivalist, the primitive
euphoria of explanation by sound, vision, coincidence. The fear
of catastrophic phenomena, illness, hunger, death. Or the need
to placate, seek totems, allies, structures for guidance. Connections,
connectors to the phenomena which inspire us with fear, joy,
wonder, discovery, exultation.
Ah, inspiration. The hiccup.

Fractal on the plane.
Again.

What do I know apart from crazy fantasies her dual life – that's
a laugh so over-simplified, neat, such categorisation as if the
complexities may be reduced to what are you drinking? Red or white?
Ah finally, when the noise had stopped, I read. I had the misfortune
to find myself reading that book. Early sixties this time, originally.
Desperate. Flaccid, a boring tedium. This woman choosing what she
must have seen as a heavily stylised manner, a rebellious, radical,
contra subject matter, such as it was. No, not at all, creaking, cracks,
without ear, tuning. Without apparently any ability to facilitate
a dynamic whole while a remarkably small vocabulary lacking
any interest in terms of syntax, phrasing, utterance, the paragraph etc.
was all that was in play. It was/is just so in that 'I presume
I'm very clever ' way. Sadly, so much paper, ink, glossiness
a nice imprint; so little promise, so unfulfilled.

So little promise, so unfulfilled. Life in the haze of doing. It could
seem there was an implicit connection. Some covert signposting.
Large phases of not being able not to be doing. Lives
reaching round. Feelings, reactions
contexts, interactions. Stimuli of languages evolving
changing dichotomies imposing vagaries
form structuring the whole. What?
Shebang!

Formulaic creed, won't happen either; as with a surfeit of
dinner or the set rota of limited menus. This fascination,
predilection for discovery , discussion of, the room, or lack
of it. The notion of time to oneself. After these years
for that to still be a recurrent theme, hemmed in by so much
industry. Of necessity, there will be more
… so quintessentially of its class/time/era.

Majority of such productions coming from post-imperialist
or presently aspirant imperialist societies,
attention unevenly given to selected short eras. Allows for undue
emphasis, shifting of register, tipping of the balance. The
weight of those busy tomes, names in print, lists of
participants; hagiography. Invented, superimposed
retrospectively. Many from of their time might say
retrogressively, if they could. Being the voice of a dead
person – that's fiction. Cheeky fiction, a chancer's game
when done purporting to outline views, attitudes, nuances
of the life undocumented elsewhere. That is not literary archaeology
it's literally arsingology. Making us so – well – pliable,
malleable, ultimately negligible. Owned away to nothing.
One blending into another becoming increasingly
featureless, personalityless as we are mustered under
the selective banners. Occluding light, deluding might.
Such a free fast way to powerlessness. Let's see, how
can I disempower you, me, her? Ah yes, block 'em all,
block 'em all in groups, under headings, allow for no
complexities, adaptations, flexibility, change. Make
it humourless, earnest, a grim tale. Stock-in-trade.
Serialise it, everywhere you can for as much of whatever
it is you can. Then bitch. On. Continue. Ok those last few do
a disservice to a minority of shrewd and excellent writers
who have never engaged at this level. However the point
stands, a minority. So, the terminally dissatisfied yet
self-satisfied earnest bleating homogenised groups gathered
under banner headlines; lacking even the everyday complexities
involvements of a family tree. Not allowed to be real,
faceted, live through differing eras; not to take
from valid work done where intelligence integrity have
mediated politics and public or academic funding has not
set or interfered with a writer's work...
be in opposing strata, participate through many cultures.
The over-simplification of the fruits of creativity, intellect,
to the point of wilful stupidity. In whose interest is this?
It's certainly easier to control.

Anything you have you carry with you. Anything you do you make.
Vice versa. No one can take away from you, ever, that which is
yours alone. A room is a room is a room. That rose. Oh
bright star. The space is necessary, it cannot be bought.
Services and locations may be bought to aid or facilitate
the tardy, unimaginative, ill-disciplined, simply
'to buy more time'. They do not constitute the idea of the room.
An idea of creative fecundity; unhindered writer given rein
(that big word again, freedom, tentatively) (never thought it
would come to this). Lots
of writers from pre such production
times understood this necessary objectivity.
Abandonment to the head. Symptomatic of our
present and recent past all re-explained
concretely, articles, items, places, jobs.
Comprehension of the mundane.
So a room it's stuck there metaphorically
any magpie concurrists' mode. Similarly echoing political
phraseology of much critic speak. Accepted codes
rarely scrutinised, a
rigorous scrutiny needed. More a slap-dash only looking for
evidence of blah affair. Tedium.
Analogy just another device.
Not quote, soundbite, device pointing out how
– works, as it delimits.

These are the facts yet this is the reality. Actuality is factual.
Factually present. Really now. How perspective is adumbrated,
shared out and reiterated, amended and exaggerated,
refurbished. These are the facts yet this is the reality. Deal
with that. Contravention in celebration, mourning,
declaration. Fantasy in white.
Some things will change.
They just may not be the ones you counted on.
Day is long and goes by fast. Flick of an eye, curl
of a lash. Hint of a grin. There is no other to do any of these
jobs. No matter how. Thralled or trawled. Least
amount, necessary. Neither do I think of
relishing the miscellaneous 'voicings for', the(ir) dependence.
Time enough

Or just examine the errors in the prestigious European
professor's canonical volume of writings on literature.
Facts awry. Figures astray. Mistakes let away with for how long?
Becoming cemented into other writings, understandings
of epochs, authors, history. The binocularising effect of the
game of telephones. The entirely unheard /unlooked for result.

Some questions and answers.

What does it say?
Volumes.
What does it mean?
What it says.
How do you know?
I wrote it.
Why did you write it? (like that?)
I read what I wrote/had written.
So, what does it <u>say</u>?
What it means.
Ok, but what did you mean?
I meant it to say what it means so I wrote it in a certain
manner for the reader to read it as such.
Why did you write it?/do you write?
I like thinking, writing, reading, making.
How do you read this?
By putting on glasses, picking up the book and vocalising on
recognising the cognizant shapes, as learnt many moons ago.
Yes, but what would you have it say?...about-?
Precisely what it does, right at the moment of contact
recognition each time every kind of reading occurs.
Ok, but you're awkward you know that?
Hmm, straightforward.
Whatever...listen, I'm looking for answers here.
I'm giving them.
Yes, but...
Just not ones you've already decided you want to hear.
But I need to know..
But you don't need me for this, you've already decided.
My role is other. Your questions predicate your answers,
which render the questions obsolete, reiterated framings for
what you yourself are perceiving.

Only listening thinking questioning discourse questioning terms
questioning parameters

Day comes. Day goes. Torrid air moves. Distant sirens cry. Horizon of brick, ledge, chimney stack, tarmac lines eating into one another. Colour bleeding perspective. Murk and grey, charcoal and wet slate, sedge and verbena. Lights changing everything moving. What is. A natural world. Which is made.

These problems of grammar, syntax. The constraints of lexis. Sedge and verbena varying through the illuminative cloud cover, sky. It made my friend fall over. Sky. She had never seen so much happening in one before.

Just as a face is a picture. Pull one. Now. This is not suggestive. Perhaps you should do that again. Light relief in the programmatic pantomime. Design.

Murk and grey, the hazy daytime silhouettes, shed in a siding, winking light on a truck. Bulk as silence, as shadow. Sentinel figures of the geocarte, necessary, solid.

Charcoal and wet slate. The green of greys. It is a true thing. Who sees? Butcher's pavement after heavy rain, raw light through the plate glass frontispiece, spilling out across dark marked squares, rectangles. An evangelical appeal momentarily. Colour bleeding perspective.

These problems of writing. Imagine monographs on aspects of art. Lights changing everything moving. What is a natural world which is made. Natural world which is made lights changing everything moving what is.

[to be sure I had not wasted my time here]
(end of OPTIC VERVE A COMMENTARY)

Holier greener wittier more erudite than thou or
just plain bitchingly cleverer than
pedants vying for attention   while
any audience wants to be... told? bossed?
patronised? bitched at? entertained? allowed
to play? make mistakes?
What is this culture fear   in which
others must not make mistakes?
Who does it seem to undermine most?
What does that tell you about empiricism
imperialism law and order the sets
of modern dysfunctunalities that so
readily trip off the tongue asked or un
is it so terrifying? real functional
utilitarian to make mistakes
learn find out it works/doesn't work
produces x or unpredictably y
has no effect whatsoever takes
a longer or shorter time uses less
or more material   becomes easier
or harder to continue/replicate/
enlarge

there is no trajectory that can speak to me more effectively
then seeking inspiration advice technical background
information whatever I am capable of finding
at a particular time in a certain context whatever can be processed
in and for that state always skewed by terminology shortcut idiolect
mind state conditioning experience wellbeing situational responses
and already proscribed delimited effectively by the notion
of whatever I set out to discover in the first place round and
round heel to the ground round we go up on your toes over
and back   that's out of whack
kiltering along

ASTONISHED BIRDS

Astonished Birds

imagine imagining
imagined monographs on aspects of art

this width stretching
vertical measures resounded well

astonished
birds imagine
art aspects of
imagining
art

waiting for that moment
clash as the ing of
any precedes its
event builds precipitates
recognising dual
qualities of är
arrhythmic
recurrence of jag
syntactical
alliance between deliberately
your more empirical
diction
and mine
so much later
coming at you
through another
language set of mores
outside us both
like it

                    cold
but not always it will
sense indoors it seems
garden
accommodates diagnosis paths conversation
oakleaf acorn rook and crow

so
realistically
checking for nits
fine comb pulling out
blonde hair
by the roots

small aquatic blue basketwork
chair child size full of
goalposts nets
of k'nex

scarves of mist dispersing over the river African violet
blooming to death possibly a cup of hot coffee wedge
of chocolate apple pudding
ploughing through job ads littered with errors
typos folder of sheet music dining room table
still attempting to requantify optically what constitutes
in the eye of the beholder perceived
mechanically programmatically in conjunction with...
in colour too
applied to realia lushness or sparseness
vegetation in the field of [   ] study
many questions unanswered   a thousand years
something to do with your hair life goes on till all hours
where slate grey wet atlantic light slopes across a granite
face glinting water drops oozing quietly out of the
thick layer of composite blanket bog saved for today in a
conservation site slaynes resting creels empty only the odd
roadside stook structures small patches
enterprisingly thatched roped down hard
winter's stockpile the heather's far from blazing in this richly
muted landscape changing hues while I think
watching twenty questions all
answers probable blown down into killary round
clew bay where all those ancestral o'malleys burkes and related denizens
of our tribe played   forays and homecomings win or lose wine
for city merchants turf wars tom making pictures by
lough corrib cong   o'malley chalice not yet dug up
life what happens go to the national museum
see it displayed   brought my kids bought the postcards
marvelled how it survived secret preserved forgotton
gone to some graves   on a boat to spain france america
food of dreams fabric of life stuff of legend
both sides of the country families dug up over
a couple of centuries artefacts that help to recreate a little
of our past carve a bit for our future sense of a
perspective it's actuality the living texture of
its remains sight of pikes wrapped in bloody oiled linen
bits of leather buried deep in a ditch smell of clay dogs

uncovering bones the strange but true fact that some of their
predecessors a couple of centuries earlier on the run too went
across to the other side of the country away from their
buaildhes in the Wicklow and north wexford hills hiding out
to the limestone and bog of connemara the granite in the heights
safe harbour wide bay rocky coves lighting bonfires on headlands
burying butter on the run or to be there on return from
buaildh'ing (how many kids even know where they put their schoolbag
at the end of summer let alone the butter) butter as wealth health
prized blood and butter milk and bread oats on the griddle
or in the black threelegged pot on the turf fire
traditions of literacy advocacy representation hard men and
women an uncompromising tenacity hard work sharp funny bones
language a tool implement of power element of destruction
a decision forced by circumstance but taken with intent stem
the tide turn the tables reopen old trade routes regain
lands knowing the so-called wild countryside like the back of
their hands each headland cattle path bog road rivulet salmon
run grove bog   generations of children reared for survival
in this new language brought up to go away work for more
other mind what they knew mind what they said.. bring it
all back home

all too familiar when compared with other relatively similar
socio-economic/political landscapes of the
modern era particularly the more agrarian societies
there's a thought same kind of racial ambivalence
towards those born outside the mother country by each of the
indigenous cultures involved X person who considers them-
selves predominantly X who happens to be part Y or Z
finding themselves discriminated against in both cultures this
is becoming the more well documented phenomenon of current
multi or intra cultural lives why? are we not hearing
what works goes right?
how is it to be maintained repeated developed?
problems reported exist   at times dramatically
horrifically I think that obfuscation of progress
however misguidedly well-meant e.g. lobbies for funding access or
quotas of representative coverage   is a mistake which allows
a divided society build on into its series of carefully
maintained segregates forward not backward change not
stagnation people not statistics   which are merely
representative   childishly easy to skew   questions arising
whose are they? why have they been accrued? how?
how is that information re-disseminated? why? by and for who?
you get it   stop swallowing

it is
real revolving
evolution
a cyclical
chromatic
pierced

sharp straight radii
long neverending
all directions

early medieval man
spread-eagled
x'ing the globe

superimposed
cut and tied
drawn lines

clown

roped into wooden
or metal curve
now up
now down
teeter totter which
way round

and the long man
castrated by
victorian decency
still proud on hill
side
chalk line downs
seemingly erratic but
tight little tracks

to seaford exceat
alfriston east dean
polegate abingdon
  any number of familiar
  names   caught in
thick fog sweeping
the small estuary
sheltering from the
heatwave half asleep right
in under the enormous
tree parsonage
garden   through
leaves   dappled day
  usual twitter and hum
 clearer level sound
an attention listening
possible this still
pollen heavy air
            listening eyes
closed   vowels from
books pass by
squinting
rustling tinted light
would she have stood so?
replace blouse with
simple shirt
waist a matter of
corsetry

chive tilts coriander
seeds flowers thinly
against the wall apple
mint spreads leaves widen flatly
no river dance no
exuberance bog
mint survives complete
neglect remains sparse
disparate

Astonished birds   in over a minor hill
post   accumulations   unrequested   couched in
fabulous colour plethora of font styles
language of birds   resuming normal paths picking worms
habitat intact nonetheless strutting carefully
along   territorial robins
daylight lingers last
clouds blown away
pale sky emulates
brightness returns
us to spring staves
off night

a sorrowful complaint
echoing its
lament   prefiguring
any musical terms
necessary to its
rendition
a ley
strange wild love song
these forms of troubled
expression pre sentimentalisation
figuring

morning would come
chairs stand at table
airways contract expand
react hearts beat feet
slide lift in some
dazed replication of
neat pugilistic
steps designed to
outwit glide sift
reflex reactions adept
at nothing the most
important fact
achieved that
nothing

Those lesser everyday catastrophes
elided in surface
tensions necessary to create
form a view a trampoline implies
bounce spring reverberation
voices used
facets of content aspects
of style items of
structure fictive
on the line while
waiting silent
ordinary alert
what is sprung
tight wire
dips sways
vibrates listen
that dog
bark part of
mind encompassing
holds sound name
action an
active nontemporal
density of particulate
ions atoms of
uncertainty chance
their charges
dance realign
mute till
surging orchestrates
through friction
movement leap
        synapses
singing

The fish which; (February fourteenth twenty ten) as nobody else either little or large, quiet or rowdy, has so far seen fit to tell the tale of, insofar as such is known, and onsofar as can be reasonably speculated, I could herewith deem a seemly topic for disimmurement or dissemination, or a quiet tale.

Let us say, the fish which regularly and with, it seemed, some notion of whimsy, tapdanced with its non-existent teeth, its be all and end all of a tail along its glass receptacle.

Or there is that same fish which regularly achieved vertical ascent to catch its food.

The fish which grew so old it paled, in comparison, to a sickly transparent pale salmon beigygrey hue, but that wasn't you.

The fish which nobody knew or could understand. As just when an action, a behaviour (termed for a series of any such) should manifest itself, become an apparent fixture or occurrence, unpredictably, it disappeared, or changed ineradicably. Such is the desire of the human brain to comprehend, understand, predict, control.

The fish which died young. All its flashy colouring still intact, vivid, aquiver with the echoes of a vehement movement, an impatient nature.

The fish which apparently, so the mass of fish world onlooking people say (aficionados?) is without personality, character, lacks the ability to provide companionship, does not have what we know as a social instinct.

The fish which came over and tapped the side of the glass with his head when child or mother spoke in the room.

The fish which leaped out of the water as a regular piece of exercise, as the officeworker stretching, child in class yawning, typist throwing back the chair to get up and stride about.

The fish which attempted to eat all of the slow release food block, in its entirety, including plastic casing which was resolutely headbutted against floor and sides in an attempt to release more munchables.

The noise that kiddo made! That mistaken belief that fish are always quiet, unobtrusive pets. Not attention seekers. Pah!

The fish which finally brought about his own demise by whacking into the side of the glass on the way back down from a severely misjudged leap. So loudly four people jumped at the dinnertable on the other side of the room and subsequently spent a couple of minutes trying to ascertain exactly what had caused the noise, a sharp, short, splat. So even as two of them had actually seen said fish leap it initially seemed too farfetched to draw what seemed to be the obvious conclusion. That the fish had hit the glass hard enough to make such a noise on the way back down.

Careless, he'd leapt so high, so free. Or a mildly eccentric fish became obsessive with a marked rigidity to its behaviour, leading to heedlessness, an early, accidental death, and ultimately, rigor mortis.

Hence, the fish which died young, having concussed itself on its own glass tank, which, needlessly, we all four people felt badly about. So, the fish which inspired feeling, lived on as a daft tale, piece of whimsy, warning. The fish which began a tale and ended a fable.

The fish which became a parable least we dismiss fables too readily.

The fish which seemed ever on the brink of casting aside his bubbles and wet, leaping out of his glass enclosure and tip-tappity walking off head erect to more adventurous pursuits.

The fish which nobody knew.
The fish which blew it.
The fish which deemed matter an inconsequential outcome of
somebody else's abstraction.
The fish which met the consequences of its own heedlessness, the
negligibility it had cast upon all that stood in its way.
The fish which fell.
The fish which landed in the wrong place.
The fish which injured itself on its own ambition.
The fish which appeared to act as if it could have a volatile
temperament.
The fish which missed its cue.
The fish which nobody knew.

Whose forbearing ancestors travelled the country in a defunct
Milton steriliser, god bless us.
Upon the lid of which rested the little legs of the youngest
family member aged four to six, god bless us.
Whose previous incarnations had been hardy creatures, longevity
a feature of their seasoned travellers' lives , god bless us.
When after a gap due to the misapprehension of the needs of
any such fish another swimmer was apprehended and duly brought
home and deposited in its glass tank, god bless us, whereupon
as has been previously recounted, despite all requisite care and
precaution, it duly died.

god bless us.
The fish which, ladies and gentlemen...
we should have tried to fit in the car.

(it's) just not cricket

is permitted
 entering stride
attempting
run out
not count
 over
call
signal dead
soon failing
attempt

damaging pitch
if there is a second
instance
procedure
indicating this
shall return

caution
as soon as
practicable
award report
reason
as is
considered
appropriate

having
ceased to
regard it
necessary
alone
decision
consultation
shall not count
distraction
ceases to be
opportunity
is required
ready
intervenes
satisfied
called
settled

so much to think   what involves the colonnade
which can no longer be seen at the drop of a hat either
no longer there or the wrong county to see it
buttressing such policies destroying cultural heritage
historic artefacts residual blanket sectarian segregationists'
affect years on budgetary constraints
conservation exploration interest consolidating present
monetary accretions rapidly still maintaining any credibility
easily succumbing success fame power
any sphere sold out bought up distorted redistributed
modified informations fly in the face of
complacency aggression manipulation arrogant manhandling of actualities
this is a mistake cannot work
actualities events of others' lives all who know what
they believe to have happened believe what they know to have happened   a matter of time before
most issues turn out emotive for some there's always one
standard non sequitur of many's the awkward moment
pros cons scams perpetrated on the compliant
constant accruing detail fitting stricture structures of massed
detail read any commentator's column we are lacking a kind of
writer voice for sustainable geographically/climatically/
culturally appropriate progress lack facilitators
pushing on stepping back holding on moving forward

bright evening
light
days after
night

cloud drifts
lifts light
asides swift
bucket
prone
thrown
contents
strewn
lucky
wagtail
walking
through

day
last of
spring
first summer
on the
way

back of
house to
front of
house all
windows
in frames
opportunities
hosted big they
gap

holding that it was conventional or arbitrary
in its origin
anorthic
viewing through an anorthoscope
samphire in the granite
perhaps looking at what
is made would elucidate
this perverse pre-eminence of
what is perceived
broken
if I change clothes
neither set are broken
put cutlery in
the righthand drawer
rather than the left
nothing has been broken
repetition from one
dominant cultural context to
another of definition by
negativity in other social
contexts seen
as a limiting
stance   perspective still
tainted with prejudice the
work (logically we must construe
for the exposition
in their own terms) so only
fitting to be talked at/about
niched as poor relation
shabby bizarre clothes odd ideas
inbetween skintone etc
it is as I had thought the
problem is not mine it's neat
teenage sadly relevant
I seem to have been growing up

wishing
in the still to
know the
way to
find the
answers even
when I did
not understand
leave soon
aerated
aerobically wretched
worn to bone
head leavening
all semblance
left tilting
quixotically
drooping as
head independently
resumes its
rigors entertains
a variation
on the
stricture
takes snapshots
filed for
posterity
repeatedly
insists
necessity of food
drink the
leavened
head how

not
to
become a
severed
personality a
disembodied
voice from
the
ashpit dump
oh whinny who
will if he

was sending postcards
still
importance
of remaining
voice
iterating
choice

the picture
chair
folding table
leg
impossible
Berthe
the weave is
rush in
textural
aplomb
we would see
you less
head turned
aside
hair loosely tied
back long
upon a green
fabric
the picture
chair
folding table
leg
impossible
Berthe

When
had I lost
sight of
the small
ovoid bird
shape
through
lens as
visual
itemisation
targeted
smaller shapes
bigger holding
areas followed
lines
closely annotating
textural
anomalies
of bark
peeling briar
clumping
nettle edge
serrating
silhouetted
shadowed
snow

world déhaché
dehiscence of time
dehiscent
volatile non dejectory
dehortation of
dehumanisation
del credere
impanation
purveyed imparity
imparkation
of what was held
common the
impenetrable
impenetrate
obdurately
imperative

oh yeah?

[to be sure I had not wasted my time here]

old head
    the ball there

he's alright

ask him
along

was going
    say

    walked
rapidly
strangely
crossed
there when
senses ambition

have borne
books made
questions
ask
silence
young
brutally
inept
solitary
pensive
compassionate
(that's one
marked down
greyed word
negative
connotations)
at that moment
wonderful
sure fire true
toiling

beautiful
night
stern
presence
    of sky
important
     perfectly
commonplace
     rage
could see it
see
capriciously
fellowship
unconventional
perhaps and this
facility
reminiscently
discreet
quiet
woman
hearing all
its changes
irrationality

intransigent
aeratesia
yr woes
belittle you

slightly
bright

what if she said sorry boys that rigorous just not
seeing off the competition get fit or what if she decided to
rigmarole pedantically as the Saturday job shunting stock
lists required for its erudition was that audition no auditory
well ignition or a view of interdite could be some cog was
missing

b for five thriving is how ye'all miss c'min' on tardy so
slow lardy as grease monkeys lets drop some spanners see
the works while clangers emit mooting less each limit bypass
ineluctable dressage eventing somewhat showily across the
greenbacks I was watching tired tiring of watching was
moving away still yet moving away again alright moving along the
harsh prefabricated sewn on after seams of nylon flight
moving past seasons surfeits repeats repeals moving through light
moving through thick slow contaminated particles might carry
some oxygen moving through fight moving through curve hastily
plane moving through dot line summation odd judgemental creatures
jumping off boxes on the sideline moving through night at last
lengthy moving towards that aperture blank moving towards sight
moving towards a fierce uncalibrated quixotic quite untold
moving walls moving signs moving streets moving quintessentially
boring kinds of time moving like alright

what day what way what
hey   the job is
what intimacy
restlessness abounds
  abates briefly sojourn
of accelerated rest
  bears no resemblance
to stopping fast by
a holding area
cleverly done with
symmetry
a lot rarely
spending every letter
on the possible
  significant
claiming irreducibly
 what what what said
  the noise was a
   sort of rattle
   and thud
critical distance
intact
looming
against green
as the least tiring
colour reduced
ineffably
to function
why light why might why
plight   the job is
why loquacity the
functionlessness surrounds
irritates chiefly milieu
of deindividualised pest

a misnomer worse hyped hope short straw held out
to need pulling the rug out smiling benignly
beckoning 'forwards' 'onwards' euphemisms
'towards us'
desire for homogeneity universality standardisation
regularisation uniformity archaic buried
in desert sands   silt of ancient sewers   seas whose waters
pirates ply little bears up under scrutiny control
money power manipulation exploitation
reasonable consensus worldwide what did not work
those dispersed who see what is not working
not enough effort resources analysing assessing
actuating actualising   dilemmas
each generation of electorates (politicians, opposing factions,
protestors, educators...) primarily investing in moving on time
for thinking systematically bred out of attempts at discourse
pertaining to any evolution of social mores   most burgeonings limitedly
programmatic   procedurally formally inaccessible a warping evident
over 25 -30 years (where are you?) product/outcome carefully
stimulated growth points nurtured   having moved from quality to
quantity 20th C   moving from quantity to rapidity   rate of attainment
(hesitating to use achievement) such are our cells

we are not there yet many fear the equality of dissent
and whole nations practically founded on it...
which brings to size
difficulties of scale, reducing levels of centralisation
could benefit implementation application of the centralisation of
others time and motion study people priorities, divergences,
not enough done meetingisation of the westernised attempting
commodification   futility droughts, wars, famines,
genocides...   could do better smaller infrastructures, less feudal
pyramidical shape to administrative powerbases
working towards making   our great and grandparents
participated in societies in constant flux
eras of dynamic change which significantly   arguably usefully   catapulted
us forward   we cannot rely on subsequent generations doing
as we would or might have envisaged however without the forward thinking
outward looking over generations I would not be sitting comfortably
writing   product of generations of nurture war trade business education   an
extended family structure existing functionally hinting at some complexities
efficiencies which the economic necessities of mass emigration belated
industrialisation have obfuscated   aware of my luck maintaining that tradition
what feeds me can feed another honest paradox of my cloak;
ní leath do bhrat ach mar is feídir leat an chontu. Nodding back at
Brehon law; don't spread your cloak farther than you can fold it.

the story of Cara and Jane
not so fast   it is not unusual
they were two people   separately motivated
intent on their hairdryers   time off
eyeliner   perhaps one was a little
fixated about her height   Cara?   Jane?
either way we can see it is possible
to make work   each from within its own
perspective   I am too short/
too tall I wish I were/were not
however   do we need these details   Cara
Jane   did such a matter exercise their
emotions so unduly with such regularity
that it is necessary for us to be
a party to it   life is easy
bliss with the occasional upset   personal
disaster of what? magnitude   here and there
(my curling tongs have blown a fuse
/parents refuse to loan me their car/
if he was a boyfriend I'm breaking it off first
/I think I'm not well/
someone nicked my mascara/
apparently the other driver maintains I
reversed into him so they won't
/my hair is flat/
did you see her dress/hair/nails/boyfriend/teeth/
shoes/car/bag...

oh unenviable Cara and Jane for a
more recent update substitute ceramic
hair straighteners   add credit
cards mobile tablet cosmetic surgery
Cara Jane   whose game do you really
think this is?   if you could just get
the made-for-TV-novel on an e-book reader
perhaps you'd get far enough in to wonder
Cara and Jane that comedian you wowed
on about was so drearily retrogressive
I could see snails getting there early/
teeth decaying as hair crackled stood on end
bristling with the repetitive boredom Cara?
Jane?   wouldn't another friend go a long way
making your lives more well interesting?
stimuli viewpoints   does that really
matter if it all hangs on the nail varnish?
how will you cope   in
whatever era   out there
alone? you know it happens
all the time   see the relevant possibilities
contract expand unbeknownst to you yet
extant ambient   latent
atmospheres of necessity   or who cares
attitudes of want dealing with oh look
what I got   the ever diminishing skill base
Cara where are you? can you motivate Jane
to move along a bit? Jane she's your friend you
seem to imply the juxtaposition of your two names
being the norm aren't you concerned about what
happens when you can no longer reach your own toenails?

the story of Bob
the lad was he lad is a bit
definitive in British English speak a little
less harsh less judgemental here even
a term of affection group of
friends the lads irrespective of actual gender/
predilection so Bob's story from a
usual name with for here a less
usual abbreviation not unheard of but less
often utilized than Rob Robbie what does
that say Bob? did you choose it yourself
or is it what parents/extended family
members designated as fitting? of course there is
always school the street it could come from
any source hell Bob you must be a
survivor tenacity there in the nature
are you aware of it? what does it take to
get out a little more from behind
Bob it seemed relatively innocuous at
the start now it's becoming a hindrance
won't they send you home? perhaps you could
put in for it plead isolation sickness
the gravity of the actual situation

well Cara Jane Bob   dismissive
generalities at least allow us access more
quickly over beyond trivialities banalities
Bob can be quiet suits him   sort
of steady demeanour not as profound mature
unusual   as an air of gravitas
a professional and it could be said social
asset notwithstanding   the nuns on the
plane the last bus home   queue
for umbrellas in the department store with the
antiquated clock outside   archaic tubular system
moving cash from central office to
register vice versa inside   diversions
across the city centre evacuating areas under
bomb threats streams of anxious
hurried commuters and dossers of all sorts on
the hop one way or the other   bound out by the same
few routes regardless of individual destinations
that idea of choice as free-for-all
who gets there first how many fit
in out on over   quiet movement
ordinary tone of Bob factual matter of fact
Cara and Jane now they get radical leave
the crowd one or both together   always feeling
they know best whilst failing admirably
in processing the situation assessing possible
options available pannick rates highly
alongside self-importance gait shows
anger disdain some hauteur say cheese!

could they be friends? who would want to know?
why any interest in them what they might
say? how long can this go on?
it is not easy to desist what if there were tendencies
inklings of Cara and Bob or Jane and Bob or
well work it out that would any of it
create sufficient friction to alter the mode
Bob Jane Cara seated in the evening sun
shining below them water laps the shores of
a badly pixelated bay too many dots for
joining simply not there this is how these
three see it quiet still lonely perhaps
adventure least we forget where is it?
the sea swipes along sandy strand stones
rattle shift settle accrue
attenuated ions the light in their eyes
inverted existentialists at large upon the green
who would be mean tolerant arrive arraign
these foreign powers a stretch more articulate
the joint with frequency   reminded of
why ostensibly we are here of Cara
Jane and Bob your uncle? shouldn't think
so   nodding ceases irregularly a
badly sprung cuckoo clock
tiring Cara Jane Bob with their
don't rain on my parade hats
on together along the winding wooded

path coppiced grove susurration of dry
vegetation crackling cinder twig underfoot
hesitancy unavoidable in the passing this
place of unique climatic zones Cara Jane
Bob walking dogs swinging along till
shelter cosy framework of shade
loitering paths resume their duties of
relaxation deviation diversification framing
desires picture Cara Jane   Bob
who are walking through pulling a dog by
the lead heedlessly transparent ambivalent
pacing a rock appears conveniently
placed for sitting peeing dogs
humans solid rock its shadow
down from one side over a bit the only
evidence of sun somewhere square
far there   light of caterpillars moving
caul of the living animated woods it's
not hard Cara Jane Bob not difficult
imagining stories sprites nymphs in
glades snakes under logs filtering
through a lazy greenish beigy mesh active
as eyelashes do you see how you fit in
the picture? what size you are? where it
all ends? blend of realisms missing
nicely how the idea of walking the dog
became a formless formulaic an antidote
dishing drama hell Cara Jane Bob you
could see how you could get to like spending time here

resuscitated evening   breeze on left
cheek tint of pink glowing   through a fricasseed
elongation of cloud backlit airy mass
rosy hues escaping ostensibly through
worn textures thin breeze on left
coastal saline sun on right intense a
little humid prickly smell of unadulterated
pine dampening dune grass yes here there
still are real dunes   there still is time
foot forward flexed toes stretched neck
turning twisting hair held back by a slender
practical hand (those nails!) the hand nails intact
trailed back through hair languid the
shoulder set of an early forties american
movie starlet   this colder air intruding
carrying voices along the river   there is a
river   trickling out down to sea
over the hill through woods across dunes ambling
all but disappearing along the way having
one last quietly assertive meander right there
down on the beach a wider point as
cliff curves back inland to make a cove
for the next headland to alleviate had
the cliff been mentioned? headland? still
it's coast you know that a bit
limey round here one side more than the other
Cara Jane Bob stirring scratching searching
the middle distance sky over sea for? boats?

water skiers? swimmers? cormorants? pushed up
now on elbows noses keen to the chill
preceding an end to evening tides to follow
dogs root raise legs people yawn
lift jackets papers dog leads hats sunglasses
water sound on shore the only loudness
round   hard perhaps even
beginning to understand Cara Jane Bob
their resolute indifference to all interest
seemingly considered élan their silence
hard perhaps listening to
that not being told why there are
questions for questions from
questions   Cara Jane Bob make three
Jane resolute unhappily dignified she
feels what?   hard done by
disenfranchised a nasty malicious bitch
of a streak condemning the development
of any instinct for sociability
to ruin a ruined expression could
say face if plastic surgery
was out of the equation anyway
expression gets there quickly implicit
psychological taints ungainly
notional displacement
it's here notice pointing out
go get on now it's here it
will take years avail of the necessary
Jane however will not acknowledge

nor be wise   will continue
to seek ways vindictively undermining
companions' joie de vivre raison d'etre
camaraderie identity even tough one
as for reciprocity lack goes with the territory
that conviction (cliché) absolutism in all
matters particularly pertaining to others
oh Jane you are a pain short of
statuesque so aware of it clumsy
lacking charm yet eager to overuse
what is there what remains
Jane Cara and Bob really seem to have been
stuck with your ever decreasing
spirals of deception awesome lack of talent
in any direction which has not
stopped you trying power hold thing
kicks you off doesn't it? you see guile
clever performance sad Jane when
the chits are down (right word) Cara and Bob
frown inbetween clowning as
they take you off   should we
introduce James about now he's been kept
out so well feel he ought to have his name
in the running   we know he shouts but
then he leaves with you a lot who
could blame him?   who could say hey James
keep it down let her manipulate weave stir
not many I attribute

some of it to junk food those synthetic
chemicals have to go somewhere
frenetic over confidentialities
propaganda feed   this Jane's no actress that would
be a boon there's no Tarzan either
way too much action for Jane who as
said before is a pain
so enough about her as Cara and Bob are
ready to move along each quietened by
the lengthening strand evening light glinting
small waves sharply breaking against
little rocks at the point of the cove look
one of the dogs has run before them left
paw prints down across the biscuit shoreline
crumbs disturbed as he lifts   runs
barking at waves splashing towards a
gull out shaking rapidly salty
coat trotting now least they catch up
are Cara and Bob calling? where is Jane/
doesn't actually like dogs as with everything
else dogs feature as accessory
or excuse which seems to allow her to feel
clever she's not there yet so Cara
and Bob follow the dog ahead intrepid
scatty at the turning tide wet with two

more following behind content to sniff paw
turn over pad along easily after the heat of
day coats stuck with burrs stickeybacks
damp sand beards of grass seed stones
embedded in the narrow path back overlooking
the strand they will go through dunes
again on into woods are those
embedded or simply worn down
to through light sandy soil absence
of vegetation evidently a much used
track even old larger
stones rounded down shiny
tinged with red tinged with blue
what is grey?   where is Jane?
don't hear them calling her perhaps they
know where she is maybe they are glad to
move ahead at a pace which
precludes any conversation with dogs
between buffer zone of sniffy fur
evening chills more Cara pulls
her jacket on fully leaves the collar sticking up
hair tousled wind buffed in her eyes
pulls on a hat the large brim
shades her eyes she can look behind
what does she see? Cara? why? one dog
eventually another coming round the
corner and Jane no Jane must
have gone back the other way it would

be like her not to say considered attempt
at dominating actions conversation
good luck to her maybe she'll fall down a
ravine hang on there aren't any (here) oh well
maybe she'll have relaxed by the time
she gets back have walked it all off
be calmer Cara resumes
her journey in the usual direction onward
as she had commenced happy having
licence to dismiss said Jane from
mind eyefuls of brilliant wet sparkling
catch attention she watches the pull
wake of tide alert to sound gull
on the crest dog on the shoreline panting
Bob 'ow'ing stumbling loose stones
pattering paws occasional nails clicking on
stone behind torpid lulls between very
quiet shushings approaching trees
nearer bird flutter water aground lapping
at the side at stone shaley stone shifting
putting weight on occasionally
cracking as they lift on/off   more
muffled crunch on the interior central area
pine needle scattered floor deeper
softer scents of vaguely musky antiseptic
summer salt pine on the tongue at the
back of the nose humidity ambient impossible
to know if it's lifting descending quiet
interlude walking cooler   extend the range

explain the aim raise the stakes the
objective becomes less pressing Cara Jane
everyone knows their names and Bob who of
course is rarely given the opportunity to feature
anywhere he's been a slave to
laziness serf to something he appears to
perceive as security likes dogs he'd have
lots if he could afford it
however nobody else he knows
wants lots   out on a limb
he doesn't like that   easier to mullach ort*
fit in he likes the walk especially now
almost out of range of the shore before they
come right under the hill he's realised his
mobile's picking up a signal he
can phone x at work rub it in status
king wouldn't you like to be here
or down the pub cool what? nothing
nobody like empty space do what you like
you know bet you're sorry you spent
yours on that encumbrance of a car now? what?
oh right a new computer oh laptop
with what sorry can't hear you breaking up...
that fecker always trying to get one up
the headland recedes a little to the left as
gulls light on small rocks at the
point of the cove the bay has a drift
a lean look of hazy indirection
each picot edged splay of tiny inlets a necessary

*sa mhullach ort (what's he mullach-orting about now?.. mullaghroating)
Tá an obair sa mhullach orm (I am pressed with urgent work)
Tá sé sa mhullach ort (He is pressed by it/it's getting on top of him)
Ta gach uile rud anuas sa mhullach orm (I am overwhelmed with everything/
everything is on top of me/piling up

part of the groove named feature in somebody's
life meeting place haunt an urge to go dig
around for the stems broken bowls of old clay pipes
thin sea breeze slants against cheeks
a little less frequently now less chill in
air still no sign of Jane all the same
he's not sorry she could be a right
pain not entirely her own fault
he supposed but no of course it was she
was in control it's Jane she sought control
dog patters on ahead assessing tree
roots no doubt finding traces of
when they had ambled through
towards the sea that morning grief! had
they been there a full day! no
wonder Jane... she's just not the sort of
no she's not used to herself
that would be a stumbling block still
life goes on the two dogs follow behind
tongues lolling panting a little coats dripping
from the midway down where they had
stood in the one deepish spot in the stream
an elliptical pool set in the first layer
of woodland where freshwater sprang
straight from between rocks fissure of
fresh sparkle cold water held in
a small concave a dell of rock worn to
bowl to pond dogs instincting towards
bones or lack thereof let's hope

they didn't come across any rabbits quiet dogs
really tired out perhaps older than the one
in front a little staid evolved to
manners in somebody's books owned of course
now there's a thought   of which we
feel sure they are not capable
dogs by the sea daylight waning night
improbable   and least we forget there has
still been no sighting of the perhaps truculent
Jane   could she have got lost? in a
serious way? should he call the
coastguard local pub her parents?
why was he falling watching himself falling
into this spring-loaded trap again? learn
learn   look at Cara and her dog
you keep forgetting Cara   they're
thick as thieves though that doesn't help
she walks well not like the other one still
there's something proud distant
nearly all the time take
today   didn't really let her hair down
she likes it here but would be
just as happy on her own why has she
come here with Jane with ? Why?
and James oh he's still to be got back
to   set in his ways no putting in a
day like this would have us think he's the
grownup   maybe that's where Jane went
didn't want to be seen coming back with

us relaxed happy   well alright tired
tousled after the day   shifting
caterpillar light in a mesh of evening beigeness
carries sound token silence nothing
spoken   nothing has been said
evening drifts as day has drifted
night provides opportunities cloaking casting
new shade   turning each tree to
lingering shadow itself extending the
slightest sound listen on held
breath night   is coming   bird on
branch balanced for night scutter of
squirrel passes by aside up a tree
branch home for night caterpillar
light evening falls silently towards depth
damp lasts in air imbues nostrils
with moss spores stays on skin alongside
roughening salt breeze odd mica glitter
particles of sand   glistening   perhaps there is
no way back   that is the answer or
an answer perhaps it is
the end that is why Jane has disappeared
alternatively gone ahead   perhaps we are lost
she actually knows where she is now
it all looks the same here under the light
canopy of foliage   night cools pollen
released hangs in air palpable
texture lent solidity duration by
humid currents   not a sound not a

sign not even a damned dog bark who
does she think she is? it's not right
not fair not playing   alright
this is sulking he reasons but it's been a long day
if there were to be some resolution
wouldn't it be   you know
best   light starts brightening shadows
lengthen narrow a way through out
shows door hall   lit
space welcoming   how we dupe ourselves
effort of recognition downplay why
should the dogs stop? is there a voice?
voices?   it's a disorientating business
this or maybe some kind of sunstroke
ferns are getting shorter sparser
clumpings   dogs all gone   on out
of sight barking to each other now and then
must know they're nearly out
at what cost such a day? or at what
cost so many of all those other unequal days?
how balance them up? achieve parity?
and Cara she has stopped before the edge
of grove nearly where a wide
swathe on the way in or out is coppiced
neat cinder pathed runs fingers through
her hair uses the brim of the hat in her hand
to dab forehead nose chin turns
smiles expectant says 'dinner now?'   and steps on in
to the tamed world the world of the Janes and
the Jameses the world of Bob she never looks back
never waits

and that lastingness doesn't translate as
durability duration span usefulness   nor as
essence of essential quality mitigating
doubt or anger   Bob's never far behind
even while physically so apart as to appear
engaged in some altogether separate
pursuit he is carefully in line only
so far as some unspoken invisible agenda
of his own allows   he wonders why everyone
bothers so much now there's Cara
heading off no notion of shortening stride
slowing pace altering her route to suit
until she wants to she seems
happy   allows her to feel
unrestrained   no proscribed route or time
scale no social admonishments her brief
lull anywhere out in air as long as
she could walk quickly enough to ensure
division distance purpose previous
additions to these outings had often viewed
such behaviour as an almost reprehensibly
positive attribute good lord there goes Cara
again! just look where she's got to already!
that hint of shock-horror envious tone
I-would-if-I-could-only about it then
there were the sideways swipes later in the pub

Cara's such an independent one isn't she!
she's got a mind of her own! this one particularly
amused Bob as a term of denigration
after all he thought inanities abound   yes
Cara got a reaction alright from that
type of slippers and pipe brigade he could
almost hear them rattling their newspapers in
disapprobation and then Cara didn't hesitate about
Jane perfectly straightforward said she didn't
like her that I know why or think I
know she would never trust a person
who has proven themselves malicious
underhand deceitful vicious in their
behaviour that Jane's a weirdly ungrownup
underdeveloped bully and I'm welcome
to her just do not let her interfere
in anything that understood
she said stick her in the spare
room till she finds her
feet otherwise she's so keen to bite off the
hand that feeds her
she'll end up lost abroad or
in jail are those people bringing her to
court for fraud? it's reasonable
they should you know she lied
for years so mundane she
must have felt so practised she didn't
need to try anymore or this one's for
you Bob she said I really don't want to know perhaps

she had grown to believe a lot of what she
put about used to consolidate her
position as she saw it on the one
hand sneering giggling maliciously a
backward child on the other parts
of that artificial self-belief   and falsely
constructed identity worn like semi-permanent
makeup lashdye   you're welcome to it Bob
she said just don't expect me to pick up any pieces
whenever the inevitable happens the
inevitable? it'll catch up with her
no one can lie stupidly all those years
without having large crevices appear just
be ready she warned   how? that's up to you what
you decide to do she hesitated said I may seem unhelpful
but am doing as much as I am
prepared to your business it
changes things   changes everything how
I view you   integrity what I choose
how much time I spend
on any of it   the degree of maintenance
I am prepared to provide how we
all use places access facilities
Bob it's a catalyst something has to give
he could hear her voice talking like that
in practically the same tones she
would use to describe a slightly complicated
bus route or the setting out of the

agenda for a meeting Cara and in
behind the Cara does   there's Cara   is
Cara walks on not particularly looking
at seeming to pay active attention to
anything legs move   rhythmically stride
adjusting to alterations in surface loose
stone leafy branch down slight inclines
muscles in her calves stand out as she shifts
weight lifting one leg over a rock
she lowers it steps on her route doesn't seem
chosen as much as happening   not many of
the more usual pathfinding criteria seem to apply
over instead of around through instead of
around or across up instead of around
still Bob maintained his position a little
aft and at only an intra-continental time-
delay somewhat preoccupied with ideas of
food experimenting with various
ways of cooking eggs achieving their
optimum state textural dilemma eggs
cooking Bob walks along Jane-less none
the worse for it   a little surprised
finding it all quite pleasant
it was not having to   Cara was making
her way on more slowly now the
light was waning making it tricky underfoot all too
easy to get a foot caught tree root
sprain an ankle worse   even trip up over

a hidden rock fall headlong Cara felt her
way ahead when she could not entirely trust
her eyes used a foot to probe ascertain assess
before she moved her whole weight forward
nothing to hear much but damply
wafting breeze through trees subdued
crunch of dewladen pine needles occasional
start of bird disturbance of stone
clacking shunting slightly water clearly
nowhere near anymore hesitant hardly
audible plash night closing more quickly over
evening here canopy safeguard from sun
rain   barrier sense of sky limited
distant darkening mass   forces of nature
readjust realign encompassing us those who look
on as much as those who might agree to
play a role therein   threatening sense
of nowhere fighting to be let out have cognizance
a confusion of directional misinformation
carried on the tail-end of that saline current
water plash very distant shorebreak muted gear
changes distinct from the far road nothing nearer
no noise to hear   if voices they are quiet meld
in the dark   if footsteps they are silent   blend
in the earth   I could stay here
in this thinks Bob now that atom of
certainty nearly caught reduced the essence
of us   each   both   neither of us
walking not calling   listening not talking

moving not going   shifting not realigning
knowing not asking   I could stay in this
other-people less airy zone marking our trajectories
quite well   happily ordinarily
    Cara is still moving knowing she will
inevitably have to stop does not prevent her
acknowledging it would be good if
it were otherwise   the human she finds
a giggle   the state of it   better
slow down allow a more natural
resumption of the journey all that
way back   loud as it would be
loud silence to be   quietened loud bodies
loud car loud road   let's see thought Cara make the foot
steps more marked don't hesitate anywhere
push those low-slung branches out of the
way let them whip snap open the path
push over large stones make way hurry
it's got to be the end of the day now here
under this inverted shade before the remaining
light before people cars fight for attention
we must have an ending building we're aware
of one we each own outright car
door closes thud in air desperation
increases the need to see be there get out
but how finish without sound without doubt
Cara smiles Bob on as he climbs a last incline
nods as hurriedly quietly she says you know I
can't waves him on through first goodbye opening

opportunity thrust which Bob inimitably
declines ignores misjudges but being Bob which
is how Cara likes him   trusts just how
it is as she does which has made such
a rare thing let no dilemma count
road roars blackly alongside ferns tall grasses
what will last perhaps only this surety
reaction of response   responsibility of action
picture of night climbing clouds darkening
what might be mild warm an extension
of the day out   car road drive
length the sleep a quiet purpose in
both and Jane? James sees to that as
usual stalwart unafraid carrying himself
intact

Bob Cara Jane now James hoojering along back
the road they came James stolidly representative
choking gear changes steering into the increasingly
misty night checking Jane's pulse nodding alright
everyone still here windscreen clearing headlights
on a modulated tone from the engine now
it's running along wider road in fourth gear
not too far an hour or so soon be near lights
traffic   action   shrugging on their poses tugging
their urbanity out   filmic quality of such
intent sees Bob struggling to balance himself
hold a semblance of that palindrome he hears
them say with such familiarity yes Bob knows he's glad it's night
a cover gimmick last bite of the apple at its height

maturity   road slows the flow of traffic
intermittent noise changes as a diesel
engine passes headed out from town towards
the coast road   scenic drive in the
dark or long way to the next town
free of junctions lights snarl-ups flow
of traffic slows this road narrow several
car lengths between vehicles a hazy
indeterminate faltering light each one paling into
the engulfing abyss of unlit route as it
reached a bend or accelerated along a
straight the late hour ensuring steady
progress lack of parked cars blocking things
up a common aim in their direction
arrow of what could be construed as
hope in some minds the getting there
(wherever...) achieving that hence
there a common equation though to speculate
on with what complete complexity diversity
of intention each individual on the road
slowing with bends slewed with headlights
embarked upon their drive to speculate
as to the full nature of their actions on each
achieving said theres is probably a
futile even more thankless task
mind out with little inkling of
its workings dangerous thing
steady   hold the course release the
elements to nature let humanity endorse

flight of reason   Cara Jane Bob James
the car runs along under arched trees whole
esplanades worth of which meet over the middle of
the road tip mingle pillarless in air
providing sheltering burrows through which all
drive a little more slowly carefully mist
in the dark looming coming out up for air
potholes of uncertainty in the longer runs giving
rise to religious prayer oh jesus let this be
the last feckin' one of these I can't see
a thing is that light the end or
only a gap on a bend   the travelling
awareness that the news carried after every
weekend an inordinate number of single
vehicle crashes into drystone walls trees
telegraph poles over ditches harbour walls
pier ends the mist moving deceptive
lightening perilously was a fucker
James concentrated sweating mildly his
eyes on the road ahead both hands
on the wheel occasional peripheral
glances at Jane who appears to sleep
in a strangely awkward position the other
three sat in the back perhaps squashed
a little queasy but happier with that
than walking these roads of tail-lights
a uniformity of habit   curving twisting
turning doubling back climbing steeply
corkscrewing sharply road of fright if
you let it take you that way or

road as king if you let it own you under
the circumstances it can but dictate in a
proscribed way but as driver passenger these
limits dictates arise in another set of
perspectives   the road may engineer their route
necessitate their compliance with certain
prerequisites of road use road user etiquette it
may inhibit or enhance their abilities as
road users according to its provenance
technology level of maintenance
popularity locale however ultimately how they as
road users choose to react to any such
enhancements or inhibitions is a matter of
some moment such a choice in reactions being
each one each our individual responsibility -
seeming to precipitate changes in cortisone
levels in the body which given
what we know of how the brain
actually works act as a catalyst to
crises - roundabout or T-junction
right-hand turn by a left side of the road
driver vice versa crises loom at
each and every juncture

he never gave up hope
cliché evident   he knew recognised simple
boorish optimism   relief in age old
adages   you will believe what you
want to believe   hence can only
change any outcome if you can foresee
predict even the probable and the improbable
possibilities   after all   what's possible may not
be likely but it's not after all completely
impossible there is a chance   risk
adventure aperture reason of reasons creating
sense of a being in motion intentional
extrinsicisms to issue forth a little new
intrinsic one from the void the fill
landslide of cause and effect reactive power
reductive film-making has tried to get
this here and there across europe he knows
this is not the same (   ) a classroom
example mirror foil but the
possibilities endless permutations of anarchic
hope that free radical travelling by in
the slipstream he knew he could try
supposed he could do some of it wanted
to do as much of it as he could
what with one doing leading to another
he could see he was off in a hack
as long as current situations prevailed
after that? what matter   things
would be different anyway life goes on
unbounded he would find a way chance
his own talent skills in
the daily fable making move myths
a little further over accommodate
pain   happy natures quick resolute
lapping ahead laughing one way or the other

to relay this he realised would be useless
what must be done   is already in the
midst of being done the achievement of moments for
each such situation resulting in the
tipping of the fulcrum   unease which alone
can make way towards new equalities
difference invigorating countenances
shading meanings   ah man you
have your work cut out for you thinks
Bob following the fading trail
car tail-lights ahead he sees Jane's
right shoulder broader than the top of the
passenger seat slouched head
lolling to the side James drives well
releases him gives time to
think he doesn't reckon he is thinking
but no one's speaking
now the hum thunk of wheels
on road steady engine vibrating
through gear changes   a rest from
all that space of time he'll have
to decide something after that how
long could it go on? Bob finds his
head nodding as vaguely he
ponders the wisdom if any of it
knows he's tired can't
remember the last time he had so much

fresh air walking all
the same day flexes his legs
carefully they seem ok a bath
later that might stall any
muscle tightness tomorrow another day what
was he to say they didn't already
know hadn't already thought of no that's
not the way go back he tells himself go
back where you were thinking about
continuing your ability to make these
places in which decisions seem
to be making themselves over time
you know it'll be too slow for Cara he
warns himself does that mean some part of
a decision has already been made
is readymade self-evident is this one of
the thorny bits he's been loath to
acknowledge he sighs Cara stirs moves
over rests her right arm alongside
his left one her shoulder warm

she'd love to sleep entirely but the
part of her mind that dealt with
waiting in bus queues laundry filing
repetitive conversations about the weather
grocery or clothes shopping wouldn't let her go
completely asleep held her
suspended as if awoken early
morning birds at the guttering
dustbin lorry small clock face showing
fifteen or twenty minutes to go
before the alarm would sound demanding

reaction her headlong participation in
events making morning light wavering
brighter across her falling eyelids at the
approach of car truck going the opposite
way light indicator of volume
both of traffic and the
estimated size of a particular vehicle
large haulage trucks lit circuses
squeezing eyelids down protecting her
state abeyance of negotiation
responsibility   lulling time   her right
side felt warm cosy she didn't want to
move anything let a draught in
from the surrounding atmosphere
Bob solid not shifting either he
felt she thought hazily as if he were
comfortable ok sitting there the
state of play cramped drive
back after the day   she found that so
predictably reassuring she had to turn
many of the day's events over
in her quietening mind   bring
herself to tiredness   seeping in
taking over how far she got
with anything   realising
reality   circumstances   how
glad she felt   Bob sitting
beside her the nagging bit of her mind
kept trying to interrupt the flow

rhythm pitch and toss of the opportunistic
game of coherence dealing with many
circumlocutions tipping readily from the
superficies of mind
in which eye she could see Bob's
face is this how you see somebody when
they are dead? she wondered a
version diluted yet ready-heated
(aliveness proximity) variant
of the grief stricken evocations mourning
can bring?   am I trying it out? now
that I know what I am at she said
to herself or is my mind reacting to
what's evolving in this ambience
of us all we create time will
tell she thought
that will be news won't it?
won't realise I'm giving it
until long after if at all I
won't have to do anything
happening skip a
step here   pop one in there jump
around a bit over there fly the
way home   could easily be song
her head felt heavy   effort of
keeping upright this she thought is
not the time to get lyrical don't
want to know what would be
made of a chorus anyhow turned into

dissenting drama motivated by individual
meaning   what significance! can't abide
that wonders if she has hummed aloud
almost spoken head feels muzzy
pervasive sleepiness stuffy humid car air
length of time it seemed
to be taking inevitability of there being
nowhere for her legs to go that avoided
contact with Bob the largest youngest
huffiest drippiest dog on her left
didn't fit in the wired off section
behind the seats with the two
older ones dog breath drip dander
probably have red
eyes swollen lids big lopsided
swollen face at best still
dogs are characters in their own
right wouldn't be an issue if it weren't
for her unnatural awareness of
Bob his foot for instance in
relation to her own wore her out
this tormented lunacy   fiction
of life   didn't like how it made
her feel   the positions she was
frequently left in resulting from others'
abeyances didn't like the glaring gaps
samenesses   this could she saw be
a major constraint choices floundering
under the weight of their addendums

sub clauses flourishing paraphernalia of
what passes for logic most of the time
evening she knew was wearing on
down thin light left as if beckoning
affectedly through treetops ditches
mist clumps James is an entity
Cara said to herself in recognition of his
stalwartness stoicism vulnerability
what circumstance changes allow James
participate more fully or is this all
there is for us what she wondered does
Jane know about this? why do they still
get on it seems well or manage
to constantly tolerate each other
beyond most people's reasoning   nice
Cara reckoned being close to such an
unpredictable practically unimaginable source
of form structure good form too (a horse)
what waste though so much
time gone she mused   hard to come by when
you wanted it in quantity
difficult to ensure fleet dour
mortality transience
insubstantiality   time   non-existence
problem pinning
any significant amount down
in the shape I need it thought
Cara then with a note of
cynical amused panic onset only stopped
at the vault she realised she hadn't
had any rest her mind chugging away
all the time Cara was not pleased
resolved that the cure for it was
to sleep at once completely
utterly with maximum resignation to the
vagaries of its states and stages

Cara is a wise woman thinks Bob fast asleep
she'll be fine when we get back
wishing he felt he knew where this
was going that would mean a lot
in his present situation he knew there
was no point in talking about his work with
this lot except he hesitated maybe Cara
though that would in his terms
spoil things alter the balance
affect momentum the interior
we bring thinks Bob
shells rollercoasters
lots to answer for he can see from
the set of James' shoulders
muscles tensing at the nape
driving remains tricky he should
have offered to do some help
acknowledge all James did start
carving that alcove he would need
to fit into still they couldn't stop now
change too late too many
cars on the road hadn't expected
that had forgotten to factor in the
new ferrylines operating from the near
port   down the coast
outlets of sanity

he decided to forget about driving
clearly wasn't suitable to start on
aware of his own tendency to get
hung up on some perceived good
idea when one came along he stretched
carefully one foot at a time
not to bang James' seat kick into Cara
still snug alongside he wondered if Jane
was asleep if it mattered to
her   could see it was
of some immediate
importance to Cara trying to
stay asleep he envied her ability
to sleep or have semi-decent
rests in all kinds of odd
circumstances why he saw her
after a dinner-party in a heatwave
heavy humid she had been
working all day he had seen her
remembered clearly sit on a
wooden chest toybox take a cushion
lie down right there curled to fit
oblivious to the noisy petering out of
party glasses clinking sudden bursts
of laughter as they say he
thought she has a mind of her own

she's not adverse to using it he decided
to try rest properly make the most of
comfort warmth close now allow
himself to drift

James drove on eyes ahead not shifting
attention off the road now the mist had
set in thickened drifting patches dense
swirling droplets condensing on the car
moving through it he knew he would
be glad to be back   out of this
ramshackle car finished with another make-
believe do-you-good hike what
did it all do he wondered
none of it seemed to make any
damn difference   everything went on
same as always regardless
as it would   on this return he
worried or thought it an
irritating matter of concern that
despite the chronological practical evidence
so far being nil for any respite
rebate any damn good in his terms
coming of this activity yet
they wanted it wanted to believe
it would help   could
alleviate pain make way
for adjustment it's not a game
thought James   never been one
losing people's not a game   gaining

people's not a game   he didn't want to
think when driving yet it did seem
to present what were good
opportunities for doing so
passengers each in their own
way allowing space to perform
this task they deemed so onerous
custodian of their lives en route
he'd find their terminally
longwinded conversations onerous he
chuckled that car up ahead
needed to keep his eye on that one
stopping starting slowing going

knowing it would take less time when or if approached in a certain way with the application of a different methodology did not mean he wanted it to take less time mentioning something a liklihood or noticing it did not necessarily have as its source intention any notion of want this he knew was going to constantly be an uphill battle with her both of them each different so strikingly dissimilar in their
reactions in such an interaction which would superficially seem to have some quality of similarity to each about them
no they were never going to be interchangeable or that commonplace no matter how he tried with a view as always to making life easier for himself blinding trees and bushes

merging into hedge here there especially
along the left-hand side change
in tune from tyres on the black
surface smoothening out consistent
hum emanating as they spun
along this newly metalled section track
cowpath   herder's delight nowhere too far
to stray   small groves copses dunes given
to sea on the right stony foothills rocky
outcrops lines of low stone walls
massively bent over trees left
blinkering the cattle effectively loosely leaving
them with their instinct for pasture an
illusion of free passage

Jane hurt she wasn't one hundred percent
sure where knew she didn't feel right
was she ill? hungover? car sick? had she
had an accident? stayed up all night?
if she could only remember
where she was had just been
who was there what the purpose was
not work that's for sure she was
wearing ancient shorts could
hear James clearing his throat was
aware of Bob shuffling round a bit behind
Cara's smell was that her hair or
who cares! ah they had been there were
on their way back still she was worn
out carsick fed up pandering to their
solipsisms Cara's waywardness Bob's waffling

ever decreasing circles of their mutual
dependencies   knowing how
they tended to view her as
the least able she liked to keep
that perception there valid
part of the group's functioning
suited while it irked   kept them all
doing their thing while not precluding
interaction as required she
had no idea of her immediate
circle viewing her any other way
as this was what she had decided
upon Jane struggled dealing with
days at the best of times felt her
life always difficult didn't
see why for instance Bob must
be included the others got on
with him better than she they said
he liked her now she tried to
conceive of why he mightn't
have prior to this nothing weighed
in his favour if he hadn't liked her
that then was a measure of his own
parsimonious nature she Jane
liked everyone! well not everyone
the same way or tried to was it her
fault those who just couldn't be told
what to do how a thing was? surely
she ought not to be blamed for the wilful

obtusity of those others the non-compliant
as Cara ironically put it whenever
they talked of these things not often
she realised it would become more
infrequent unless Bob were diverted
perhaps he could take up something
time consuming   suitably
physical which neither James nor Cara
would be interested in devoting
time to   these notions underlying
attitudes crept around her mind as
she neither lay nor sat in the front
passenger seat beside James
all the way back she did not seem to
notice react   small conversations
comments about the route   the undeniable
tedium it was being drawn out to
drifting sea fog traffic Jane was
as Jane is concerned with Janeness

looking out at sunlight
through eyelids Cara thought
was redeemably the best feature of such
trips one to hold on to carry forward
enjoy the rest tramping exploring
she liked but tramping for the sake
of it exercise   taking minds
off their troubles not her thing
too often instigator motivator
it had been wearing thin for
some time she thought when would
it be done for her? certainly
hadn't happened yet James was the nearest
thing being competent doing
his job fairly in the context no
other impetus that she could tell
Bob went along with things followed
on didn't irritate as Jane did she
had noticed he was more
assertive was it enough she
wasn't sure of getting to step
back concentrate on other things
in mind or if it simply meant he
was comfortable becoming blasé

her eyelids registered another short
stream steadily moving traffic going
the other way she wondered whether
the undoubted flickering eyes
beneath their lids thinking through
these things people as the
opposing currents of car lights
streamed past had come to anyone's
attention Bob most likely
to realise she could hardly rest though
she thought James could see enough
in the rear view mirror if he
chose probably not in these
conditions she mused he was a
conscientious driver
she had first noticed
liked him for   James   the car night
sea fog closing drifting opening
amassing again other vehicles
lights this secondary route narrow
no outright danger
Jane in the front no doubt

unhappy picking holes yet there
long day ending petering out
this hazy density of water particles
ineptitude of relationships which
an outsider would deem
exclusive feel excluded from
no doubt most would retreat with alacrity
after a nominal amount of time spent at
a hotel table with us grinned
Cara they'd only have entered feeding
off Jane that need to be validated
by the world

counter rhythm had started there
a constant in the background
softish underlying swish slight
squeak minor thwack of course
windscreen wipers Bob said to
himself fog must be changing as
we get inland turning to drizzle
local variations in weather
never ceased to amaze
finding a ready source
of delight in those vagaries of
climate sudden shifts and lifts a

fascination to him following these often
minute discernible changes stretching
his legs wondering if Cara had actually
been asleep all the time could be
a way of keeping them at bay
creating distance he thought she
certainly seems to do that
with me   dripping fog
depositing water blobs on
windscreen side windows
smaller globules slowly trickling
down glass no smell of damp
in the car he realised James must
have put the heater on low
cancelling out moisture

strange what smell could elicit revivify
he mused almost understanding some tilting necessary
feeling just trying to think about damp
still he was actually too comfortable
relaxed for that to stretch
thought far enough encompass necessary
layers cores chords there's one he thought
core smell chord modified and
modifying essential essence clad in contextual
humours the naming game for those involved
in creation manufactory damp of
internal floors wet on warm days damp
of the fire bedded down for night with
dark turf damp of near visible miasmas
floating out upwards on opening
disused wardrobe doors damp harbinger
of pain stiffness swollen joints
knuckles lopsided   mould laden
congestive properties of such tonal bouquets
their graded attributes ranked to the forefront
against their so called unknowable
unverifiables even when those are facts
not statements facts feck it he said to
himself I should be writing all this down
I'll forget it later when I have to move
something about waiting travelling
proximity of mental/emotional distance
thinks Bob enabling me
is it just not having to do
anything?   minefield

why feel so unnecessary? am I he
grasped at coherence realising I am
disenfranchised in this sub
set of relationships/ at sea
as ever neat in self-sufficiency?
gawd! why spoil it? rest
of the journey to go just
luxuriate wait it'll all change
soon as we land in   dynamic quavers
at the lawnbreak pavement no object footpath
negligible front door well   negotiable
his body sighed   he felt it   nothing audible
he was sure so only Cara knew surely
she was awake just biding time almost
makes her like all the rest in a
general sense   he could view that as
reassuring ordinary approachable
or predictable tedious   swing out of
that one   leaders he thought whoever
dreamt up that category word
the roles   there's manipulation

James slowed the car perceptibly a
questioning noise in his throat distance he
thought distance that one doesn't know what
they're doing   next they'll
have stopped dead because they think they've
missed a turnoff glancing to his left
checking Jane's semblance automatically all ok
no visible change perhaps she's
actually dozed off one fewer...
his right leg was getting tense
slight pinch in the upper thigh back of
the calf this stopping starting crawling along
straining eyes into constantly shifting
drifts of fog aware he found his shoulders
hunching muscles tightening endeavouring
peering into the missing middle distance

it had felt right the outset bringing them home
being the driver packing everyone in getting it over with
now he just wanted to be finished Monday
looming sense of being crowded out of some
legitimate space around himself his activities
did Cara know she snored? all that back of the throat
semi-adenoidal texture in the air great voice Cara
if they ever got back could all be forgiven
managing to turn the evening round singing
telling stories   he liked it absolved any need to
converse respond in predicated ways
allowed interactions throughout
what the hell is that guy up in front doing?!
hardly moving more lights torches? walkers?
what's? shit! someone's been knocked
down he said out loud cars crawling round
a bunch of people lit by torches one car's
headlights there's feet on the ground edge
of yellow oilskin should I stop no what's behind has to
keep getting by keep the road moving to clear how

else get a doctor or ambulance here? do I have any first-aid...

    James James Bob's voice urgent
hissing   James it's an accident are you ok?
I'll take over if you need me to Bob knew
his offer was belated thought he ought to try
James didn't appear to pay any attention
gaze never leaving the route as he steered
carefully negotiating slippy terrain on the
extreme righthand edge of the road

I don't know what this must seem like from
outside   some looper insistent
route more important than life
no point stopping there cause more
problems   though there are those few
yep glancing up out taking the
registration supposing some
kind of negligence of duty
there is no actual obligation
to stop stare stay   no witness in
this vehicle no medic no room
to get round it if stopped the
patently latent running towards
the erupting volcano into
the path of flying debris fire
choking heatdust pelting stone
lava a tirade to come   this hand that
hand win some
whose right choice right? wrong? this does
not presage balance impute
strategems denoting   what
the hell!   why pull out
now? in front of me! gobdaw! eejit!
amadán of the highest order!

jeez! us! 6 minutes odd how long
can this go on before the battery dies?
this carry-on reduces it to almost nothing
should just work! nothing left on bar standby
ridiculous plastic metal waste
time   waste   doodle on that
(the ladybird) still conversation can
exist static in air blinding cracklings
smote wasn't keen on how things seemed
released to the inevitable
relieved of responsibility
or tone   prevalence of expectation over
matter received exegis over
evident   hence a squealing   toiling
sneering superciliousness supersillyality
astonishing to behold representation
as opinion ↔ shoving being shoved towards some
belief type orthodoxy some presumed known
mindset of hierarchy codding
themselves they're alright what is
this lack rage the experiment
rethink markers reset timers
eliminate those proscriptions most
indulged as they enable such carefully

eked out elements proliferate
  too long   beyond any natural
span as actual catalyst back of a bus
or long distance train pub party go to blazes!
she used to say now I understand
some facetiousness only worth
passing by briskly

if this dark would end the car might stop
streetlights bleakly flaring out of fog house
lights dimmed by distance curtained off
from fog chaos the well ordered
machinery with its glitches
cars parked outside sliding past dozens
    slowly   no way in or out
apparent no light   should be   not
wanting to notice the driving or James
others verbosity round such incidents
enough to know when there is no way
to do   move on pass by make room for
more of which some inevitably
end in ditches too whirr   swish
pothole thunk volume change as
road surface reappears headlights on
tarmac veering to concrete   hum
of neutral   handbrake squeak
engine stopped

looking up at the house
he saw a bedroom window
blind tweaked aside
for faces to show
against backlit glass

home again home again
jiggetty-jog
plinketty-plonk
by the time he deposits
recumbent forms on
sofas chairs   pours
drinks   opens up
the verandah for
air   tunes up begins
again   the session
carrotted as reason
motive to be there
tired a bit
sad close to the
most necessary thing
for now hardly wanting
to know   acknowledgement
from experience
involving trial
by fire   working or
the torture of the wheel
spun to light to
shut up to endure
to separate to
prefigure while
extemporising on
that notion of being
state   futures
luminosities
taste friendship
realism   life
and other
obstacles

www.ingramcontent.com/pod-product-compliance
Lightning Source LLC
Chambersburg PA
CBHW080406170426
43193CB00016B/2827
* 9 7 8 1 8 7 2 7 8 1 0 5 1 *